I0116418

~ To My Dragon ~
Happy Birthday

May all your dreams
come true.

- Love, Mommy

Mia couldn't wait to go home after school today. She was eager to open her 12 envelopes. There were 6 white, 3 pink and 3 red ones that had *"To Mia"* written on them by classmates.

She was excited because *Valentine's Day* was only two weeks away and she could already tell that it was going to be very special.

Mia ran to her room and grabbed a pair of scissors from her desk and sat down on her bed.

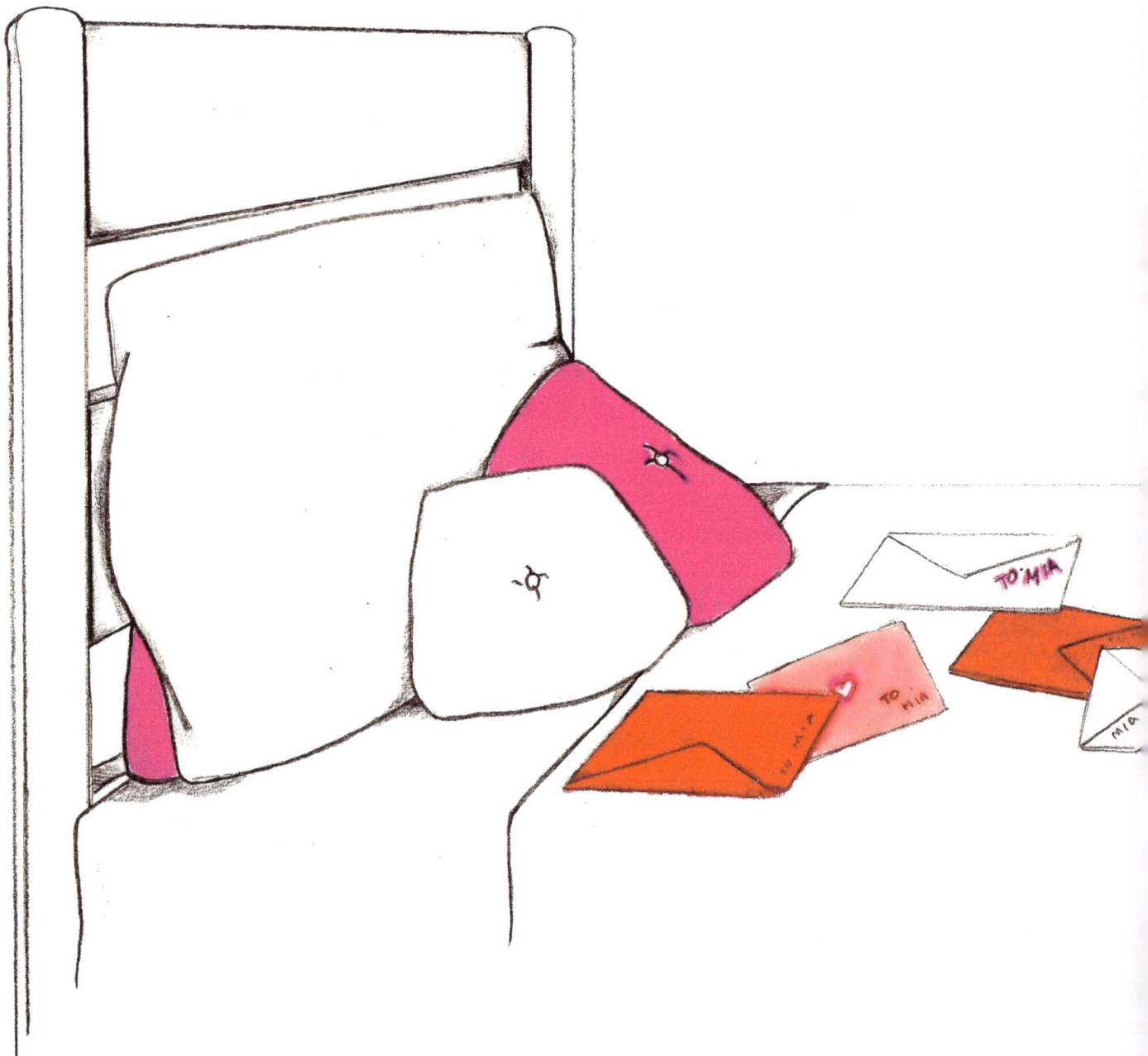

As she scattered her bounty in front of her, a red card with golden foil and a funny looking monkey caught her eye. It was the prettiest card and it had something inside!

Mia decided to save that one for last.

$\mathcal{M}$ia took her yellow craft scissors and tucked the blades inside each lid to open them very carefully. As they opened, Mia took out the contents one by one.

Mia began to open the white envelopes. The first one was a *Mickey Mouse* card, the second one was *Donald Duck*, the next envelope had a paper heart colored in crayon, another valentine was made of construction paper, and the last one was covered with glitter that scattered all over her comforter.

They were all very pretty, so Mia decided to decorate her bulletin board with the cards so she could look at them every day.

After hanging up eleven cards, she sat on her bed and opened the last one, a golden red envelope.

Out fell three coins with holes in the centers and Chinese characters written on the front and back of each coin. Mia peeked inside the envelope, looking for a card.

She slowly pulled out a slip of paper that said, *"Mia, please come to my house for a party on Sunday at 3 o'clock - Ling."*

Mia began bouncing up and down on the bed with excitement because she had been invited to a party. Ling was her best friend in school and Mia couldn't wait to go to her house!

Exhaused from jumping, she then lay down on the bed to stare at the cards. Mia started dreaming of all the chocolate candy, cakes, and cookies decorated with hearts that would be at the party.

Mia just loved *Valentine's Day.*

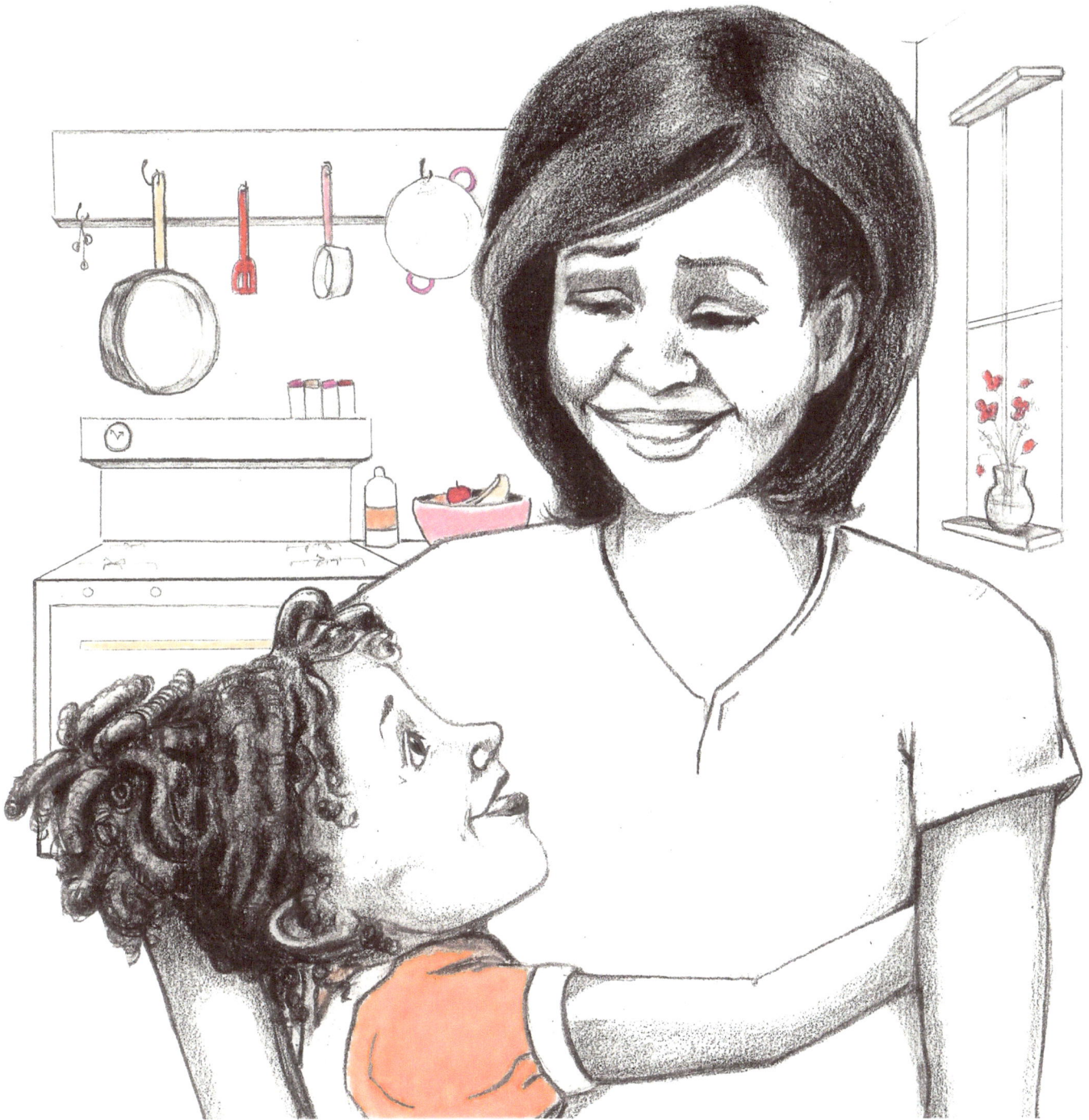

When she stopped daydreaming Mia ran downstairs to the kitchen where her mom was fixing dinner.

"Mama, Ling has invited me to her house for a party on Sunday, please can I go," she pleaded.

"I'll need a new dress and..." she said, while still catching her breath.

Mom knew Ling's parents and she often shopped in their neighborhood market.

"Well, you are becoming a big girl now and a lady has to look her best! I suppose we can go shopping Saturday," her mother replied while stirring the skillet.

"Mia, help me set the table for dinner, and we'll find you the prettiest party dress. You'll be a *Southern Belle*," her mother said confidently.

After dinner Mia ran back to her room and got ready for bed. She lay staring at her bulletin board filled with cards and wondered who was coming to Ling's party.

Mia eventually fell asleep dreaming about her first big girl party.

Saturday morning couldn't have come fast enough. Mia jumped out of bed and got dressed in her favorite pullover, tights and sneakers.

She was ready to go shopping when she heard her mother calling her name.

"Mia!"

She followed the sound of her mother's voice until she reached the living room, where her mother was on the telephone.

 "Mia, I am making an appointment for you to get your hair done at *Pansy's Beauty Salon*," her mother whispered as she held the phone to her ear.

$\mathcal{M}$ia's eyes grew larger as she imagined her hair being done in curls.

"Mom, can I get a big girl's hairdo, I'm too old for those *Shirley Temple* curls," she said as she plopped down beside mom.

"I'm sure Pansy will know what to do, just don't cut it," her mother replied.

Soon the two of them were off to the mall and Mia was thrilled to be surrounded by stores that had many shades of red decorations, hearts, balloons, and boxes of chocolate in their window displays.

Mia was drawn to one store that had a beautiful red dress with a satin sash.

Mia tugged at her mom's hand and said, "Mom I found it, this is the one!"

Inside, they went to ask the lady at the counter if she could try on the dress in the window.

"Yes, little lady, the dress is right over there," said the clerk, pointing to a rack where the dress was hanging.

Mia held her breath as her mom rumbled through the dresses looking for the perfect size.

"Here it is," her mother said while holding up the dress in front of Mia.

Mia grabbed it and ran for the dressing room.

Mia stood in the mirror modeling the dress and smiling. "I am going to be a *Southern Belle* in this dress," she said to her reflection.

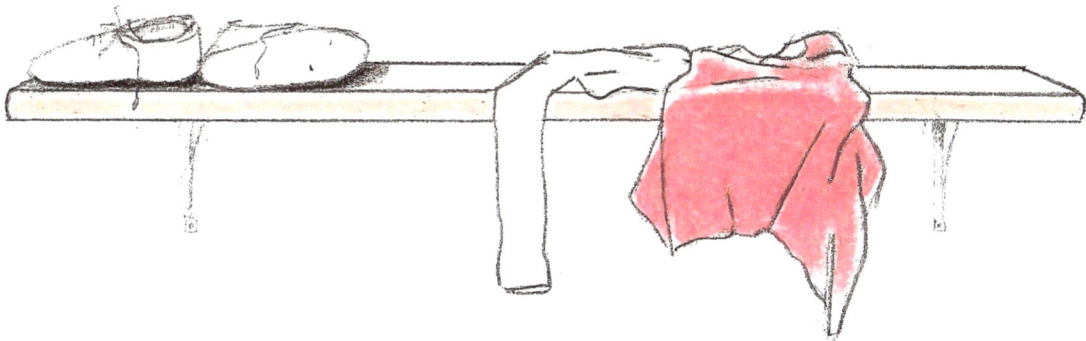

After the shopping was done Mia sat in the back seat of the car, holding the package with the pretty red dress as they drove to *Pansy's Beauty Salon.*

Pansy greeted Mia's mom who eagerly stated, "Miss Pansy, Mia is ready for a big girl hairdo, no curly curls this time, and please don't cut her hair."

Before heading out the door her mom added, "I'll be back for her at around 3 o'clock."

"I'll be sure to have your princess ready," Miss Pansy replied with a drawl.

Then Pansy sat on a barstool and started taking Mia's ponytail down.

"So Miss Mia, just how would you like your hair done today, like *Beyonce* or *Mariah Carey* or one of those *Divas*?" Miss Pansy said jokingly.

"No, ah, ah, I want to look like Miss Mia…no one will recognize me if you make me look like some *Diva*," she responded seriously.

Following a shampoo and conditioner, Miss Pansy pulled out the flat iron and curlers.

Mia's hair was long and it flowed to her shoulders. Miss Pansy only curled the ends and her temples. She indeed looked like a little princess with just a bit of *Diva* style.

That night she was careful to wrap her hair in a satin scarf before bedtime to ensure it would still look great for the party the next day.

The next morning Mia wore her new dress and shoes to Sunday School. When church was over her mother drove Mia to the Wong's house.

"Let me take your picture...oh, and be sure to take plenty of pictures for me," her mother said as she handed the small digital camera to Mia.

Mia walked to the door and rang the doorbell.

When the door opened she heard voices speaking Chinese and she saw people sitting in the living room.

As her eyes went around the room she noticed a lot of Ling's family members, but no classmates. No one she knew was there to see Mia's pretty new dress or fancy hairdo.

When she looked at the dining room table she saw a spread of food. There were big dishes, little dishes, and then a cake and many pastries on platters!

Yet, there was not a single box of chocolates, red hearts, or pink frosted cupcakes anywhere in sight.

When she walked closer she saw that the cake was in the shape of a dragon, and said *"Happy Birthday Chi!"*

"Chi?" she said with a curled up eyebrow.

Mia was thoroughly confused.

Then Mia's head turned in Ling's direction. "What happened to *Valentine's Day*?"

"What's *Valentine's Day*? It's *Chinese New Year*! The *Year of the Dragon* and Chi's birthday too!

"Didn't you get my lucky money: the three gold coins from China I gave you?" Ling asked with a disappointed look on her face.

"Oh, was that what that was?" Mia responded.

"*Yeah!*" "In China the *Year of the Dragon* is a *lucky year* and my big brother is turning twelve today."

"My grandparents came all the way from China and mom said I could only invite one friend and I decided to invite you because you are my very best friend."

"You look really pretty in your new dress. And you wore lucky red!" Ling said with joy.

After Ling explained things, Mia felt so special that she no longer cared if anyone from school was there or that she was going to have *Dragon* birthday cake, *moon cakes,* and something that looked like her grandma's smothered pigs' feet.

Mia was happy to be at her first big girl party and she was proud to be a *"Special Guest."*

She felt like a special valentine after all...

A Dragon Valentine.

A Dragon Valentine
a dragon heart

Written by Rochelle O'Neal Thorpe
Illustrated by Katy Loutzenhiser
Edited by Fatimah K. Asghar

ISBN 978-1-935706-03-8
Library of Congress Number 2011901172

No part of this book may be reproduced or transmitted in any form
or by any means, electronic or mechanical, including photocopying, recording,
or by any information storage and retrieval system,
without permission in writing from the author and publisher.

Copyrighted June 29, 2011
TXu001754323

Wiggles Press
books for the hands of little readers
Cambridge, Massachusetts

Printed in the U.S.A.

Author

Rochelle O'Neal Thorpe is inspired by exploring life through the eyes of her children; Nathaniel, Misha, and Gabriel and daughter-in-law Mary.

Rochelle has a Master of Arts degree from Emerson College, School of Communications and a Bachelors of Business Administration from the University of Massachusetts, Isenberg School of Management. She also minored in Chinese Language and Literature. She has studied Japanese at Harvard Extension School and Showa Boston. She is conversant in Chinese, Japanese and Spanish.

Catalog of Works; Captain Remarkable (2004), Gabe and the Park (2006), Gabe and the Bike (2006), The Doll at the Christmas Bazaar (2008), The Tales of Teacups (2010), The Tales of Cranes (2010), Gabe's Nantucket Adventure: Daffodil Dogs and Cars (2010), Gabe and Storybooks (2010), A Dragon Valentine (2012), Dolly's Winter Surprise (2011), Snowman in Central Park (2011), Aisha's Gift (2012).

She hopes all her works will be published and enjoyed by children around the world.

Illustrator

This book is uniquely illustrated by Katy Loutzenhiser who co-authored and created the artwork for Solaka, the Girl with the Long Blue Toenails. Katy delivers detailed etchings with spot colors that provide a dreamlike experience that will delight young readers.

Her minimalist style of using only soft colors against a black and white pencil is reminiscent of mid-century art popular in picture books and magazines like the New Yorker. This second published book definitely provides an impressive start for the maturing artist.

Katy works primarily with pencil, charcoal and oil paints, taking special interest in portraits and cartooning. She studied under art professors Mark Wethli, John Bisbee and James Mullen at Bowdoin College. She has also pursued training at the Art Institute of Boston, Art Institute of Chicago and at the University of Barcelona in Spain.

Asian Language Books/ISBN

A Dragon Valentine (Chinese)	978-1935706038
Gabe and the Park (Chinese)	978- 1935706618
Gabe and the Park (Japanese)	978-1935706632
The Tales of Teacups (Chinese)	978-1935706250
The Tales of Teacups (Japanese)	978-1935706557
The Moon Creeper (Chinese)	978-1935706243

CD Audio Books available for:

Gabe and the Park (Japanese)	978-1935706632
The Tales of Teacups (Chinese)	978-1935706250
The Tales of Teacups (Japanese)	978-1935706557
The Moon Creeper (Chinese)	978-1935706243

www.ingramcontent.com/pod-product-compliance
Lightning Source LLC
Chambersburg PA
CBHW060839270326
41933CB00002B/143

9 781935 706038